DREAMS ILLUSION and other REALITIES